The Golden Role

iContractor3

The Golden Role

Just Be Nice!

iContractor3

jon m ketcham

The Golden Role - Just Be Nice! – iContractor3 by jon

© 2016 by **Jon M. Ketcham**. All rights reserved.

No part of this publication may be reproduced or transmitted in any form or by any means, mechanical or electronic, including photocopying and recording, or by any information storage and retrieval system, without permission in writing from author or publisher. The exception would be in the case of brief quotations embodied in the critical articles or reviews and pages where permission is specifically granted by the publisher or author.

Disclaimer: The Publisher and the Author make no representations or warranties with respect to the accuracy or completeness of the contents of this work and specifically disclaim all warranties, including without limitation warranties of fitness for a particular purpose. The fact that an organization or website is referred to in this work as a citation and/or a potential source of further information does not mean that the Publisher or the Author endorses the information the organization or website may provide or recommendations it may make. Further, readers should be aware that internet websites listed in this work may have changed or disappeared between when this work was written and when it is read. Please see following page for additional disclaimer.

ABIYD Publishing Company
765 Park Ave
Meadville, PA 16335
www.ABIYD.com

Cover art / logo by: Jon M. Ketcham

ISBN: 978-0-9905511-3-3 paperback
Library of Congress Control Number: 2016900046

10 9 8 7 6 5 4 3 2 1

Motivational & Inspirational / Metaphysics / Mysticism

First Edition Printed in the United States.

Additional Disclaimer

The information and strategies provided by **The Golden Role** are intended to educate, inform, empower, amuse and inspire you on your personal journey towards excellence: goal-setting/goal-achieving, growing your business/bank account, achieving optimal health/wellness, improving your relationships and maximizing your quality of life. It is clearly not intended to replace a one-on-one relationship with a licensed health care professional and it is definitely not offered up as a substitute for proper medical or chiropractic advice, diagnosis or treatment. Proper diagnosis and advice relative to treatment of any existing health conditions cannot be made through a book and is well beyond the scope of any information offered. The intent of the author is solely to offer information of a general nature to assist you on your quest for spiritual and emotional well-being. The author will not accept any liability, perceived or otherwise, for the improper application of any principles taught through this text. In the event you, the reader, choose to use or apply any of the strategies in this book for yourself, which is your constitutional right, the publisher and the author assume no responsibility for your actions.

Just Be Nice!

Dedication

For Lisa

Birds and animals that live on a lake flee when the lake runs dry. But the lotus that grows on the same lake will die with the lake. Thank you for always being my lotus. I have always loved you.

Just Be Nice!

Table of Contents

Disclaimers   iv, v

Dedication   vii

Table of Contents   ix

Preface   xi

Chapter 1   Being Born Again –
The Zero's Journey   1

Chapter 2   Buyer BEWARE:
The Law of Attraction's DEADLY *Secret*   7

Chapter 3 Can Compassion Be Taught?   13

Chapters 4 – 10 Compassion Cells

Chapter 4 In Search of Forgiveness   17

Chapter 5 Out of Business   25

Chapter 6 Going Label-free   29

Chapter 7 Mortuary Science   53

Chapter 8 Steps & More Steps   65

Just Be Nice!

Chapter 9 Call of the Wild	69
Chapter 10 Can You Hear Them Now?	71
Afterward	*75*
About the Author	*79*
Connecting to dr. ketcham	*83*
Permissions	*85*
Sources	*87*
Bibliography	*89*

Preface

So many gods, so many creeds,
So many paths that wind and wind,
While just the art of being kind
Is all the sad world needs.
Ella Wheeler Wilcox

Imagine a world where everybody looks out for one another without regard to race, religion, nationality, gender, orientation, socio-economic status and any other artificial methods currently in vogue for creating division amongst one another. Treating others as you would want them to treat you, also known as the Golden Rule or the ethic of reciprocity, is the common thread found wound through every major world religion. What if everybody loved one another, treated one another, like all the holy books instruct? What would life look like if everybody actually followed the Golden Rule?

Written as the follow-up handbook and workbook to The "Zero's Journey", this book is the passionate attempt of one semi-enlightened man to awaken others to humanity's desperate cry for loving compassion before it is too late to save us all.

Just Be Nice!

Chapter 1

Being Born Again – The Zero's Journey

...unless you are born again, you cannot see the kingdom of heaven.
John 3:3

You must be born again.
John 3:7

What does it mean to be born again? Perhaps it would be helpful to first clarify what being born again is not. Being born again is not something you get to just decide and declare. You could just as easily decide and declare that you are an automobile or an airplane. Merely deciding and declaring something does not make it so. Being born again is not something you pay lip service to for acceptance or club membership either. It most assuredly does not give you "preferred" or V.I.P. entry in to some afterlife party. Being born again does not make you in any way better or 'holier than thou' than anyone else. In fact, here is a pretty reliable litmus test for being born again. If being born again does make you feel better or more important than anyone else, not only are you not truly born again, it is a pretty clear sign that you are being an elitist jerk.

Just Be Nice!

*Learn to die and you shall live,
for there shall be none who learn to truly live
who have not learned to die.*
Book of the Craft of Dying

Being born again is about being reduced to absolute zero, as described in <u>The Zero's Journey</u> and the Biblical <u>Book of Job</u>, and then rising up from the ashes of who you used to be, like the Greek mythological phoenix, freed from and devoid of the former limitations imposed by your EGO. Being born again is the aftermath of letting go of all of your attachments, shedding your labels, dumping your baggage and living in to your own God-given Divinity. It represents an awakening to the interconnectedness and the interdependency of us all, recognizing that we are all ONE and none of us is any more, or any less, valuable than the rest. Being born again is about embracing everyone with loving compassion without stopping to judge whether or not they deserve it. Anything else is just another excuse for following your own selfish, self-righteous agendas.

Sometimes, being born again happens voluntarily; it is certainly a noble goal to strive for. More often than not, however, it comes about traumatically. Nothing awakens you to the suffering of others as readily as suffering for yourself. For that reason, being born again is usually ferociously resisted and its actual incidence throughout the populace is relatively low.

There are two beautiful human beings whom I would like to compare and contrast through their individual journeys to being born again, through the fires of hell, into the accidental enlightenment of loving compassion. Both suffered through the atrocities of multiple concentration camps during the time of the Holocaust; both somehow survived; and both found a way to create some shred of meaning from their experience, in order to help others, and became celebrated authors. Their names are Viktor Frankl, author of Man's Search for Meaning, and Elie Wiesel, author of Night.

Viktor Frankl was mostly an optimist. Even after having his original book manuscript, his most prized possession, his life's work, which he had brought with him to the first concentration camp, destroyed, he began the arduous task of rewriting it on any scraps of paper he could find. He looked for ways to find gratitude in every day camp life. And he visualized himself standing on stages around the world speaking to packed auditoriums. Viktor Frankl sought and found meaning while still a prisoner of the concentration camps.

Just Be Nice!

According to his book <u>Night</u>, Elie Wiesel, on the other hand, did none of those things. He was quite young when he was first taken prisoner. In his own words, "I did nothing to save myself…It was nothing more than chance." (1) It was not until after being liberated from the concentration camps that Elie Wiesel was able to create some sense of meaning, some urge to help others, from his experience.

> *It is not only what we do,*
> *but also what we do not do,*
> *for which we are accountable.*
> **Moliere**

I used to think that Viktor Frankl's positive approach was why he survived when so many others did not. But, Elie Wiesel seemingly did none of those things and also survived. And, it is most likely that there were others who, like Viktor Frankl, remained positive yet still died anyways. Two radically different approaches, polar opposite responses, that ultimately had the exact same outcome. Both men had plenty of good reasons to become hardened and bitter. Neighbors, people they once called friends, remained silent to their plight. In fact, the whole world remained silent to their plight for a very long time. Elie Wiesel wrote, "how naïve we were…the whole world did know and remained silent…Human suffering anywhere concerns men and women everywhere." (2) Both men contributed immeasurably to the awakening of us all to loving compassion for one another through their writings.

There is no one "correct" path, or even a best path, to enlightenment. That would imply that other paths are wrong and who are we to judge? There are just a multitude of paths to choose from with no guarantees for any particular outcome. Both Viktor Frankl's and Elie Wiesel's paths ultimately led to loving compassion for others. And, perhaps, all paths eventually wind their way around towards such. Heaven knows I hope such. Our survival as a species depends upon it.

Everybody who traverses the zero's journey towards accidental enlightenment reaches a point where they must come to terms with their aloneness. Most, if not all, of their "friends" and family have abandoned them. And, despite their best efforts, the Calvary never came to their rescue. God/Source/Universe has seemingly turned a blind eye to their situation and a deaf ear to their cries for help. Life is indifferent to their plight.

Yet, out of great humiliation and insignificance, loving compassion can bloom. Perhaps, through the kindness extended by a stranger, hope can reemerge. The Calvary may not have come with bugles blaring, but a gentle touch, a warm smile, a non-judgmental acceptance and embrace can be life saving to them. Other times, maybe just out of a desire to spare others, to be that kind stranger they themselves never received, can be all the impetus they require. Whatever the case, the phoenix that arises from the ashes of loss, suffering, humiliation and despair is one that readily recognizes the suffering of others and is no longer capable of sitting idly by in indifference.

The same smoke hovers over all our heads.
Help each other. That is the only way to survive.
[advice given to Elie upon entering Auschwitz]
Elie Wiesel (3)

When it comes right down to it, we are ALL alone. Most of what happens happens by chance. The best way to have your prayers answered is by helping answer the prayers of others. The best way to increase your odds is by actively working to increase the odds for others. If each of us did this for others, ALL of our prayers might actually get answered too. The Golden Rule tells us to treat others as we would like others to treat us. This is the **Golden Role** for all of us.

Chapter 2

Buyer BEWARE:
the Law of Attraction's
DEADLY *Secret*

*It is impossible for a man to learn
what he thinks he already knows.*
Epictetus

When we talk about "Laws," we are making reference to the fact that, for a given set of circumstances, there should be a predictable 100% probability of an expected outcome. Anything less than 100% and we are reduced to fluctuating, random probabilities, not laws. Furthermore, laws typically cross multiple disciplines. In other words, a law that causes a specific outcome in one arena usually causes predictably similar outcomes in other arenas.

As was discussed in The "Zero's Journey," the Law of Attraction, which has at its core a belief that like attracts like, is really no law at all since nowhere in the known, natural, physical world does like attract like, not in the field of physics, not in the field of chemistry and not in the field of biology. Perhaps the Law of Attraction could be useful as an analogy, a formula or blueprint, for improving human behavior. But, as also pointed out in the aforementioned text, the Law of Attraction is in direct opposition to the ancient wisdom and teachings found within numerous highly revered, holy and spiritual texts including the Holy Bible, the Bhagavad Gita and the secret wisdom of the Dzogchen found within the Tibetan Buddhist precepts. Are we really like anti-magnets that somehow defy the laws of physics to attract like? Or, are we actually all earth-bound travelers of light who emit our light and love to others, so that they might reflect back to us? It was for these very reasons that the Law of *Reflection* was proposed as a more realistic explanation of the nature of reality. Like may not attract like, but like DOES reflect like.

> *Sometimes people don't want to hear the truth because they don't want their illusion destroyed.*
> **Friedrich Nietzsche**

However, by far the biggest danger fostered and perpetuated by the Law of Attraction is something far more sinister, something that can lead to deadly consequences and has been used as justification for just that, time and time again throughout the course of human history. If you repeat a fairy tale often enough, with enough conviction, it starts to look and feel like an apparent truth to the masses, even though it is still false. *"Everyone knows that like attracts like."* By perpetuating the lie that whatever circumstances anyone finds themselves in, they have *attracted* them through their prior thoughts, feelings/emotions and actions, the Law of Attraction fosters judgment, condemnation, intolerance and indifference towards the plight of others. **The Law of Attraction is completely devoid of loving compassion!** Bad things can, and do, happen to good people, even people who follow the "laws." The Book of Job tells us this is so and the experiences of over six million Jewish people during the time of the Holocaust, thousands of Native Americans during the settling of America and thousands upon thousands more Africans during the time of slavery prove it to be true. Attempting to blame any of the aforementioned as having *attracted* their situation is not only untrue, it is incredibly inhumane and unconscionable.

As the Law of Attraction has approached cult-like fervor, it has devolved into a mainstream, propagandized approach for people to feel good about themselves and the pursuit of their selfish whims, while completely divorcing themselves from the plight of others. It promotes judgment and intolerance under the guise of empathy, an awareness of the plight of others (so one does not attract similarly), yet it is totally devoid of compassion, actually caring about the plight of others. Labeling others as savages, sinners, non-believers, terrorists, infidels, low resonators, low lifes, losers and so forth, enables empathy while simultaneously inoculating against compassion; "they get what they deserve," making it ok for others to suffer because of their erroneous ancestry, heritage, race, beliefs and/or actions; for not conforming to a feather like the rest of the flock. Such mass hysteria fuels our flock-like instincts, triggering distrust, anger, blame, and condemnation of any who are seen as being of a different feather.

People readily buy into the divisive dichotomy of this *we/them* mentality. As long as *we* can separate ourselves from *them*, *we* think we are afforded some level of immunity from *them* and their problems. However, if *we* get too close to *them*, *we* might catch what ails *them*: their bad luck, their failure, their homelessness, their unworthinessness and so on. In other words, if *we* get close enough to *them* to realize that they are no different from us, then what is to protect us from a similar fate? This backwards, closed-minded thinking blocks us from extending compassion to *them* and from acknowledging that, in reality, there is no separation such as *we/them* anyways because *we* are really all ONE.

The Golden Role

*Those who are able to see beyond the shadows
and lies of their culture will never be understood,
let alone believed, by the masses.*
Plato

When I wrote iContractor1, I made reference to an annual homelessness night that used to take place in my hometown to bring attention to the plight of the homeless:

In my town, every year, they hold a "homelessness night" where people can come and experience first hand what it's like to be homeless for one night. While I can certainly sympathize with the plight of the homeless, this event is far more likely to create more homelessness than it prevents. Having nearly been homeless myself, after the third time I went broke, I can tell you that teaching people how to think, feel and act homeless is not the solution. Far better would it be to bring in someone who had gotten themself off of the streets to share what their thought process was that enabled them to overcome homelessness. Teach people how not to become homeless in the first place! (1)

I was WRONG!!! You don't *catch* homelessness by acting 'as if' because true homelessness includes paralyzing FEAR and an overwhelming sense of utter HOPELESSNESS. Both Mother Teresa and Gandhi ministered to and served the poorest of the poor their whole lives,

Just Be Nice!

yet neither one ever joined them because their actions were driven by LOVE and COMPASSION. And, as noted in <u>The "Zero's Journey,"</u> the highest, noblest use of the Law of Reflection is in overriding our 'reflective' tendency by intentionally choosing to recognize the Divinity within others, particularly those not yet aware of it within themselves. Imagining yourself experiencing the plight of others, walking in their shoes, will NOT "attract" similar circumstances to you but not being able to imagine it WILL block you from connecting to your humanity.

Chapter 3

Can Compassion Be Taught?

*True compassion is understanding that
Darkness is Darkness and not judging
the circumstances that turned out the light.*
Lisa M. Ketcham (1)

Rabbi Harold S. Kushner, Biblical scholar and author of <u>When Bad Things Happen To Good People</u> and, more recently, <u>The Book of Job – When Bad Things Happened to a Good Person</u>, examined the Biblical <u>Book of Job</u>, paying particular attention to the earliest known Hebrew rendition. After dividing the book into its two distinctly different stories, a poem bookended on each side by a fable, he then went through line-by-line attempting to understand the author's original intent.

At the beginning of the poem, Job and his friends share a deep, intellectual knowledge of God. However, by the end of the poem, after undergoing unimaginable personal loss and suffering, Job is awakened to an experiential understanding of God that defies words and far exceeds his friends' ability to even comprehend. Rabbi Kushner considered the final verses of the poem, Job 42:5-6, critical to understanding the

Just Be Nice!

entire book. In correspondence with him, I wrote the following:

Dear Rabbi Kushner,
In my humble opinion, the entire poem appears to be a story about Job's Dark Night of the Soul which resulted in his shedding of his EGO and then his subsequent "enlightenment" as he moved from an intellectual knowledge of God to an actual experiential understanding of God. As such, is it at all possible that the final words of Hebrew could be translated thusly:

I reject all that I thought that I was (EGO) and, having experientially, intimately met God, realize that we are all connected, we are all one, and now have compassion for everyone, having recognized my own individual insignificance.

Rabbi Kushner replied,

"Dear Jon,
I find your interpretation of Job **totally plausible**."

Awakening to loving compassion occurs in a very similar manner. One can be taught about loving compassion and really develop a comprehensive intellectual knowledge of what it is. But, the only way to truly awaken to an experiential understanding of loving compassion is to learn to feel it with your whole being, letting it fully consume who you once thought you were. Loving compassion is all consuming or it is nothing at all. It is for this reason that I say, **compassion cannot be taught, but it can be learned**.

Empathy, which is defined as an awareness of others' feelings, needs and concerns, can be taught; and, it is a good first step towards loving compassion. But, awareness of the plight of others, by itself, is not enough. As pointed out in Chapter 1, there were plenty of people during WWII who were fully aware of the plight of the Holocaust victims, yet chose to do nothing in response. Moving to a place of actually caring about the plight of others is a whole different level of concern. It demands action rather than just passive awareness, looking out for others instead of just shielding yourself. Awakening to loving compassion elevates your understanding to where you can see that the only way to truly and effectively shield yourself from the plight of others is by taking action to reduce the plight of others, much like you would hope others would be moved to do for you if you were in similar circumstances.

No act of kindness, no matter how small, is ever wasted.
Aesop

Loving compassion has to be felt in the soul; it requires interactive action. And the primary barrier to entry for loving compassion is the EGO. For as long as you allow yourself to feel, in any way, separate and superior to your fellow human beings, or any living creatures, you cannot feel compassion for them. Pity? Yes. Compassion? No. Pity is actually worse because it further magnifies our perceived differences. Learning loving compassion involves getting yourself first into a state conducive to learning. It mandates becoming EGO-less and label-free, more aware of our similarities than our differences, and awakening to an appreciation that while "I am" small and insignificant, together "we are" one.

Chapters 4 – 10 are each set up as separate compassion "cells" or exercises to help you on your journey to loving compassion. But make no mistake about it. Merely reading and studying the exercises will not make you a more loving, compassionate person.

Chapter 4

In Search of Forgiveness

What is hateful to you, do not do to your neighbor. That is the whole Torah; all the rest is commentary.
Talmud, Shabbat [Judaism]

Make a list of every event where anybody has ever hurt you in the past. It does not matter whether the hurt came from somebody you knew or somebody you did not know. Be sure you spend adequate time compiling this list. No slight is off limits here. Include every incident you can think of where somebody let you down, regardless of the reason.

Was it…

- Something they said?
- Something they failed to say?
- Something they did to you?
- Something they allowed to happen to you?
- Something they did not do to you?
- Promises not kept?
- Promises not made?

Just Be Nice!

The Golden Role

Just Be Nice!

The Golden Role

Before reading any further, be sure you have at least three to four dozen events listed.

Just Be Nice!

The Golden Role

Now, you might think that the next step is going to be to forgive each and every one of the people involved in the above events. And, in a way, you are correct. Your task now is to first forgive yourself for your participation in each and every one of the above events. Much like you cannot allow anyone else to love you until you first love yourself, you cannot forgive and extend loving compassion to another human being until you first can extend it to yourself either.

In forgiving yourself, in each and every one of the circumstances you listed above, you are not taking on responsibility for the actions of another. But, you are accepting responsibility for carrying any of them forward. In so doing, you may have allowed yourself to turn solo performances into life-long operas. Ask yourself have you ever behaved similarly to others? Hurt people hurt people. Even if you have not carried the abuses listed above forward to others, have you forgiven yourself for the events happening to you in the first place? Forgiving yourself also includes letting yourself off of the hook for not being able to make your past different than it actually was nor your present different than it currently actually is.

Go back to the list you just compiled and, event-by-event, go through and try to put yourself in the shoes of those who caused you harm. Is it not possible that they were doing the best they could at the time, given their background? Age? Experience? Lack of good role models? So many people go through their entire lives denying forgiveness to themselves and others for events that really were not about them in the first place. Is it not possible that everyone listed above, yourself included, was doing the best they could at the time? Can you find it in your heart to forgive yourself and then, by extension, them?

> *Anyone who claims to be in the light but hates a brother or sister is still in the darkness.*
> **1 John 2:9**

Chapter 5

Out of Business

*Regard your neighbor's gain as your own gain,
and your neighbor's loss as your own loss.*
T'ai Shang Kan Ying P'ien [Taoism]

Take a drive through your town and find some businesses that have gone out of business or closed recently. Stand there, or while picturing them in your head, and try to understand the following:

- That was somebody's dream.
    - One they took a lot of risk for.
    - Maybe it involved extra schooling.
    - Perhaps they took out loans from a bank, family & friends.
    - They likely had to fight the naysayers in following this dream.

- This dream died.
    - Maybe due to poor choices.
    - Maybe due to the economy.
    - Maybe due to health issues.
    - Maybe just because.

Just Be Nice!

- Imagine the collateral damage.
    - Marriages dissolved.
    - Children who lost respect for their parents.
    - Friends & family defaulted on.
    - Friends & family no longer speaking to one another.
    - Credit ratings ruined.
    - New bad habits like excessive drinking.

- Perhaps you used to be a patron.
    - Perhaps in their struggle, they raised prices too high.
    - Maybe you were once offended with poor service.
        - Can you forgive them?
        - Can you forgive yourself?

- That person whose dream failed and now lays in ruins wanted the same things you want:
    - Success.
    - Ability to provide for their family.
    - Lifestyle.
    - Control over their own destiny.

The Golden Role

- What if that person was your father or mother?

- What if that person was your son or daughter?

- What if that person was you?

- Can you remember a time when things did not go the way that you planned? Where something you hoped for, strove for and truly cherished went away despite your best efforts. How did that make you feel at that time?

Just as I am, so are they; just as they are, so am I.
Sutta Nipata [Buddhism]

Just Be Nice!

Chapter 6

Going Label-free

I am a stranger to no one; and no one is a stranger to me. Indeed, I am a friend to all.
Guru Granth Sahib [Sikhism]

Start by making a list of everything that sets you apart from your:

- Competitors

_____

_____

_____

_____

_____

_____

Just Be Nice!

The Golden Role

- Colleagues/co-workers/classmates

_____

_____

_____

_____

_____

_____

_____

_____

_____

_____

_____

Just Be Nice!

The Golden Role

- Neighbors

Just Be Nice!

The Golden Role

- Friends & family

Just Be Nice!

The Golden Role

Next, make a list of all the labels and titles you use to describe yourself. For instance:

- Activity Roles:
    - Husband/wife
    - Boyfriend/girlfriend
    - Father/mother
    - Occupations/careers/student
    - Hobbies

_____

_____

_____

_____

_____

_____

_____

Just Be Nice!

The Golden Role

- Trophy Roles:
    - Academic degrees/schooling
    - Awards
    - Accolades
    - Prior accomplishments

_____

_____

_____

_____

_____

_____

_____

_____

Just Be Nice!

The Golden Role

- Physical Attributes:
    - Height
    - Weight
    - Body-type/build
    - Nationality
    - Race
    - Gender
    - Orientation

_____

_____

_____

_____

_____

_____

_____

Just Be Nice!

The Golden Role

- Belief Systems:
    - Religious affiliation
    - Philosophy
    - Political orientation

_____

_____

_____

_____

_____

_____

_____

_____

Just Be Nice!

The Golden Role

- Physical Possessions & Material Accumulations:
    - Homeowner/renter
    - Business owner
    - Fancy cars, boats, jewelry & money

_____

_____

_____

_____

_____

_____

_____

_____

Just Be Nice!

The Golden Role

Now, without using ANY of the previously listed labels, answer the following question:

Who are you?

Describe yourself in detail.

_____

_____

_____

_____

_____

_____

_____

_____

_____

Just Be Nice!

The Golden Role

How does this make you different from anyone else? How does this make you similar to everyone else? List the similarities.

_____

_____

_____

_____

_____

_____

_____

_____

Just Be Nice!

The Golden Role

While we all have unique gifts, traits and capabilities, we are all much more alike than not. At some level, we all want the same basic things:

- Survival
- Food & water
- Shelter
- Love
- Community

Scratch off every single label you have circumscribed your existence by, cast off all of your limiting beliefs, and just whom are you left with?

_____

_____

_____

*Not one of you is a believer
until he loves for his brother
what he loves for himself.*
Forty Hadith of al-Nawawi [Islam]

Just Be Nice!

Chapter 7

Mortuary Science

This is the sum of duty: do not do to others what would cause pain if done to you.
Mahabharata [Hinduism]

Particularly in the Western world, people live under the grand delusion that death is not their individual, ultimate destination. Regardless of a person's age at death, the question is always, "What did they die from?" It is as if knowing the answer to that question could somehow spare them from their own unavoidable demise. That is the only thing known with any certainty though; everybody must die! And, it does not matter whether they die young or old; it never seems to be enough time. In the blink of a cosmic eye, it is over for us all.

If you were to die today, what would that look like? Remember the lists you compiled of everything that set you apart from everyone else in the previous chapter? And, what about the lists of labels? How much value would any of those attributes and labels be to you now?

Just Be Nice!

The Golden Role

Make a list of all the things you think you cannot live without. What sorts of attachments rise to the surface?

- People?
  - List them and explain how & why you are attached to them.

_____

_____

_____

_____

_____

_____

_____

_____

Just Be Nice!

The Golden Role

- Things?
    - What are they and why are they so important to you?

_____

_____

_____

_____

_____

_____

_____

_____

_____

_____

Just Be Nice!

The Golden Role

- Outcomes?
    o What sorts of outcomes are you trying to control?
    o What will happen if things turn out differently?

_____

_____

_____

_____

_____

_____

_____

_____

Just Be Nice!

The Golden Role

- Life?
    - What are you most afraid of losing?

_____

_____

_____

_____

_____

_____

_____

_____

_____

_____

Just Be Nice!

The Golden Role

Which, if any, of the above attachments would hold any value to you whatsoever now, in light of your imminent demise? Which ones do you really think you can take with you when you die? Any?

Now, imagine the pain you would experience if you were to lose all the above, everything that you are currently attached to, but without dying. What must that feel like to lose it all, to have everything you value taken away from you? What does that do to your sense of self-worth? Does it impact your sense of fairness? Are you still able to scrounge up any hope for a better tomorrow? Such is the case for many hundreds of thousands all around you every day. The homeless, those displaced by natural disasters, refugees and any imprisoned in concentration camps as prisoners of war are the easiest to recognize. But, remember the compassion cell exercise from Chapter 5, Out of Business? Many of your neighbors likely fall into this category as well.

I am not advocating for giving any of your stuff away. But, can you imagine, even if just for a moment, what that level of loss does to a person? Can you also get any sense of what that level of liberation might bring? This undoubtedly is the

Just Be Nice!

hardest exercise cell. Humbling yourself by coming to terms with the relative insignificance of your attachments to your life, the insignificance of your life itself, is probably the biggest step you can take toward becoming an enlightened, compassionate being.

> *Do not do unto others whatever*
> *is injurious to yourself.*
> **Shayast-na-Shayast [Zoroastrianism]**

Chapter 8

Steps & More Steps

*In everything, do unto others
as you would have them do to you.*
Matthew 7:12 [Christianity]

In <u>The Zero's Journey</u>, I wrote about the essential, sequential, 3-step process that helps to facilitate accomplishing lasting, positive change and growth. Furthermore, I demonstrated how the 3 sub-steps included within step three of this 3-step process could be utilized for weathering calamity and loss. Now, it is time to see how this same template could be useful while journeying to an awakening of loving compassion. Everything you do from this day forward can be modeled upon and measured against this template.

Summarizing the essential, sequential, 3-step process:

1. Know Yourself

    Label-free: this is not about what you did, do or have. This is about who you be!

Just Be Nice!

2. Love Yourself

    This is about 1st forgiving and then loving yourself exactly as you already are.

3. Improve the World

Then, summarizing the 3 sub-steps:

    3a. Decide "WHAT" – [tangibles]

Decide to awaken to your humanity.

Decide to extend loving compassion to yourself and others.

    3b. Up-level "HOW" – [intangibles]

How others feel about themselves.
(Remind them of their humanity.)

    3c. Act "as if" – [strategies]

Act "as if" our survival as a species depends upon it.

__Just Be Nice!__

Chapter 9

Call of the Wild

One should treat all creatures in the world as one would like to be treated.
Mahavira, Sutrakritanga [Jainism]

Volunteer to help out at a wildlife rehabilitation center. This is not the same as a humane society. Wildlife rehab centers are unique in that they are solely focused on the needs and wants of the individual animals in their care. These animals are all struggling to survive, and many of them aren't going to. Your role there, in addition to helping the staff to care for the animals themselves, is to come to an awareness, understanding and sensitivity to the wants and needs of the individual animals. They do NOT want to be somebody's pets! They want to survive. They want adequate food and water, shelter from the elements, safety from predators, love and community. They have all gone without one or more of these and known want. And they want these things how they define them, per their individual species, NOT how you might want to define them for them. When it comes right down to it, they want the same things, albeit in different formats, as you do.

Just Be Nice!

Francis of Assisi said, "If you have men who will exclude any of God's creatures from the shelter of compassion and pity, you will have men who will deal likewise with their fellow men." How people typically respond to anything is how they usually respond to everything. In order to learn true loving compassion for everyone, first practice extending loving compassion to the multitude of creatures that share the planet with you.

> *One going to take a pointed stick*
> *to pinch a baby bird*
> *should first try it on himself*
> *to feel how it hurts.*
> **African Yoruba Proverb**

Chapter 10

Can you hear them now?

*Try your best to treat others as you
would wish to be treated yourself,
and you will find that this
is the shortest way to benevolence.*
Mencius [Confucianism]

Go spend time being with the homeless. Go there without any of your labels and titles. Talk to them. More importantly, LISTEN to them. Remind them what it feels like to be human. Resist casting judgment. Remember the phrase, "there, but for the grace of God, go I." The reason this exercise was saved for last is to help ensure that you have awakened sufficiently and strengthened your compassion muscles enough to be successful at it.

Mother Teresa served all without regard for their particular faith. It is said that she never tried to convert anyone to her faith whatsoever. Rather, she ministered to the poor, attempting to live her life as a living example of how Jesus lived. She encouraged her fellow workers to do the same.

Your role is NOT to teach, preach or give witness to anything or anyone. You are NOT there to patronize or condescend to anyone. You are

Just Be Nice!

NOT there to rescue anybody except for yourself. Odds are that the homeless are already far more awake to loving compassion than you are at this point. You are there as their student and servant only. Your role is to seek for the Divinity within each and every homeless person you encounter, to uncover their humanity before your own eyes, so you can learn to love them with compassion. Consider what makes you worthy of the homeless spending their time with you? Take them fresh socks and buy them a meal. Ask yourself why fresh socks, something most people take for granted, are such a treasure to someone living on the streets.

> *See first that you yourself deserve to be a giver,*
> *and an instrument of giving.*
> **Kahlil Gibran (1)**

The homeless are no different than you or I. If they still seem to be, go back and re-do the prior exercise cells as many times as it takes until you see more similarities than differences. The truth of the matter is this: the reason compassion cannot be taught is because it already resides in the hearts and souls of every one of us. Your task is simply to learn to awaken compassion in your own heart and soul. Once you do, you and humanity will never be the same.

The Golden Role

Develop your loving compassion muscles and then go out and lift up the world!

*The corner-stone of the temple is not higher
than the lowest stone in its foundation.*
Kahlil Gibran (2)

Just Be Nice!

Afterward

Non-proprietary

There are some authors and teachers out there who claim proprietary rights to their programs concerning the development of compassion. Such is not the case with the exercises in this book. There can be nothing proprietary when it comes to developing loving compassion for ourselves and others. If, in fact, we are all one, then anything which awakens us to that fact and brings us more together belongs to us all. Awakening to loving compassion for ourselves and one another is the best chance we, as a species, have for survival. But, it does not come easy for most of us. Far easier it is to choose to drown out the suffering of those all around us by busying ourselves with self-absorptive pursuits. Hopefully, the exercises provided in this workbook will help you get and stay on track.

At some point in time, in each one of our lives, we will all experience the bitter taste of failure as well as the savory sweetness of success; the vulnerability of weakness as well as the gift of inner strength; the fragility of illness as well as the radiance of health; the emptiness of abandonment as well as the nourishment of love; the paralyzing effects of fear as well as the faith-building effects of courage; the poverty of ignorance as well as the well-spring of new knowledge. We all hope to spend most of our days on the right-hand side of this equation, basking in abundant success, strength, health, love, courage and knowledge. However, the only guarantee in life is that NOTHING is guaranteed!

Sometimes, the best that we can hope for is to first learn to truly love ourselves, as we already are, and then to love everyone else, as we have learned to love ourselves. That is the greatest gift we can give, to ourselves and to others. After all, if we are all made in the image and likeness of God, as it tells us in Genesis 1:27, coming to a full recognition and appreciation of who we, and others, really are, is an awakening of the highest magnitude. And just maybe, as more and more of us awaken, the anguish felt by those cycling through failure, weakness, illness, abandonment, fear and ignorance could be better buffered and utilized for transformative awakening of society as a whole instead of as a soul-crushing sense of defeat and hopelessness.

The Golden Role

When any one of us falls, we all fall. But, when any one of us awakens, we all awaken. We are all connected to one another, whether we recognize it yet or not. When you find yourself on the left- hand side of this equation, know that you are not alone AND that there is *always* the light of dawn after the dark night. When you are fortunate enough to find yourself on the right- hand side of this equation, give thanks for your abundance AND look for others to share it with. (1)

His Holiness the 14th Dalai Lama, the spiritual leader of the Tibetan people, has been quoted as saying that his religion is kindness. I love that! That is the Golden Role in a nutshell. Why can't we all just be nice?!?

Just Be Nice!

About the Author

dr. ketcham was in private practice as a chiropractor for over seventeen and a half years. He was asked to contribute a quarterly philosophy column to his hometown newspaper, The Meadville Tribune (circ. 12,000), in the Active for Life supplement, from 2009 until 2013. Prior to that, as part of a 10-year long collaborative effort by all of the local chiropractors, he contributed articles once or twice a year to The Meadville Tribune's monthly HealthBeat column. Additionally, he is the author of iContractor 1, which he published in 2012, and The Zero's Journey, which he published in 2014.

dr. ketcham delivers a powerful message of taking personal responsibility for your results in life and changing those results by changing yourself from the inside-out!

"In order for things to change and improve, you don't need a 'change of venue.' What you need is a 'change within you'." (iContractor 1, p. 42)

However, when it comes right down to it, dr. ketcham is the first to acknowledge, "I am nobody; no better, no worse than anybody else. I am just doing the best I can with the resources I find before me, just like everybody else." In fact, rather than puffing out his chest and touting his credentials, he prefers the simple title of "jon," as he aspires to serve as a dream re-kindler to his fellow earth-bound travelers of light.

Much like Job from the Bible, jon has known more than his fair share of adversity and misfortune. Having gone broke 3X within 4 years, nearly dying from a life-threatening illness and skirting perilously close to homelessness, he immersed himself into a decade-long study of personal development and success that included reading over 100 classic works, repeatedly listening to more than two dozen audio programs and watching over a dozen videos. He was then able to turn his life around and build the "waiting-list" chiropractic practice of his dreams, only to have his entire livelihood mostly evaporate following sweeping insurance company reductions in Pennsylvania in 2012 that took most of the fun and ALL of the viability out of private practice. By documenting his journey into hell and back, he leaves a trail of light to illuminate the way out for others still lost in the abyss of darkness.

jon lives with his wife in "wooded bliss" surrounded by 35 acres of dense forestland in Meadville, Pennsylvania. He has two beautiful, gifted children: a twenty-one-year-old son, who is a talented science fiction author/artist and an eighteen-year-old daughter, who is a pursuing a career in chemical engineering. He shares his home with one Basset Hound, one Chihuahua, ten cats, a cockatiel, and chickens! Nearly all of his pets are "rescues."

jon's articles have been well received and are also available by following his blogs at:

**www.TheZerosJourney.com
and
www.AlwaysBelieveInYourDreams.com.**

Just Be Nice!

Connecting to dr. ketcham

Websites:

TheGoldenRole.com
- Coming Soon!

TheZerosJourney.com
- Follow The "Zero's Journey" Blog

AlwaysBelieveInYourDreams.com
- "Book the Doc" to speak at your next event!
- Follow "Doc's Blog"

Facebook Pages:

Facebook.com/thezerosjourney

Facebook.com/drketcham

LinkedIn:
Dr. Jon M. Ketcham

Just Be Nice!

Permissions
(Listed in order of 1st appearance)

I would like to acknowledge the following publishers and individuals for permission to reprint the cited material:

- Excerpts from NIGHT by Elie Wiesel, translated by Marion Wiesel. Translation copyright © 2006 by Marion Wiesel. Reprinted by permission of Hill and Wang, a division of Farrar, Straus and Giroux, LLC.
- Copyright © The Nobel Foundation 1986 "Elie Wiesel – Acceptance Speech". Nobelprize.org. Nobel Media AB 2014. Web. 12 Dec 2015.
- NIGHT by Elie Wiesel. Copyright © 1972, 1985 by Elie Wiesel. English translation Copyright © 2006 by Marion Wiesel. (Hill and Wang, 2006) Originally published as *La Nuit* by Les Editions de Minuit. Copyright © 1958 by Les Editions de Minuit. Used by permission of Georges Borchardt, Inc., for Les Editions de Minuit.

Just Be Nice!

Sources

Being Born Again – The Zero's Journey
   (1) <u>Night</u>, Elie Wiesel pp. vii-viii
   (2) The Nobel Peace Prize Acceptance Speech, Elie Wiesel, December 10, 1986 AND <u>Night</u>, Elie Wiesel pp. 118-119
   (3) <u>Night</u>, Elie Wiesel p. 41

Buyer BEWARE – The Law of Attraction's Deadly *Secret*
   (1) <u>iContractor1</u>, Dr. Jon M. Ketcham p. 24

Can Compassion Be Taught?
   (1) <u>The "Zero's Journey"</u>, jon m ketcham p. 132

Can you hear them now?
   (1) <u>The Prophet</u>, Kahlil Gibran p. 28
   (2) <u>The Prophet</u>, Kahlil Gibran p. 52

Afterward – Non-Proprietary
   (1) <u>The "Zero's Journey"</u>, jon m ketcham pp. 131-132

Just Be Nice!

Bibliography

Bibliography

Gibran, Kahlil. *The Prophet.* Alfred A. Knopf, 1923.

Ketcham, Dr. Jon M. *iContractor1 - Constructing Your Perfect Life by Remodeling YOU from the Inside-Out!* New York: Morgan James Publishing, 2012.

ketcham, jon m. *The "Zero's Journey" - iContractor 2.0 - A Modern-day Survival Guide to Weathering Accidental Enlightenment.* Meadville, PA: ABIYD Publishing Company, 2014.

Kushner, Harold S. *The Book of Job - When Bad Things Happened to a Good Person.* New York: Schocken Books, a division of Random House, Inc., 2012.

—. *When Bad Things Happen To Good People.* Schocken Books, 1981.

Wiesel, Elie. *Night.* New York: Hill and Wang, a division of Farrar, Straus and Giroux, 1958.

Wiesel, Elie. *Nobel Peace Prize Acceptance Speech.* The Nobel Foundation, Oslo: Nobelprize.org, Nobel Media AB 2014, 1986.

Just Be Nice!

www.ingramcontent.com/pod-product-compliance
Lightning Source LLC
Chambersburg PA
CBHW021133300426
44113CB00006B/405